SELFISH GRIEF

REDEFINING HEALING AFTER LOSS

MALIKA SABÄN WILLIAMS

ISBN: 979-8-9994744-4-5
Printed in the United States of America
First Edition: 2025

DEDICATION

Danny…my love, my best friend, my answered prayer.

Though our time together was far too short,

your presence continues to light my path.

This book is a tribute to your life,

your love, and the short dream we built together.

With love,

Lik

TABLE OF CONTENTS

PART 4: LEGACY

It all started with a painted rock...
and one very sweet question.

FOREWORD

It amazed me how one defining moment can both shatter your world and have an everlasting impact. This is what happened the day Danny died. We were together when she received the devasting news that the love of her life had died. Apparently from a heart attack. One moment she went from a kiss and goodbye to preparing his funeral. From saying goodbye and see you later to the silence of your home.

A crucial moment that would change her life forever.

The wailing sound she made is still etched in my memory. She was numb, confused, and at times, in sheer disbelief.

Once we arrived at the hospital. We were ushered into a room along with the hospital Chaplain. As we walked towards the door, there was an overwhelming sense of calmness with her. Once in the room, she simply nodded. She was ready to see what awaited her behind the wall.

It was a moment of amazing strength, courage, and fortitude. A defining moment.

Grief has a way of changing us, of rewriting the stories we thought we'd live. Yet in the pages of this book, Malika invites us to see that grief, though crushing, does not have the final word. She writes with honesty, vulnerability, and courage about the darkness she walked through and about the light she slowly found again. This is not a book of easy answers or neat timelines. It is a testament to the resilience of the human spirit, to the power of faith, and to the truth that joy can return, even after unimaginable loss.

In this book, Malika doesn't just tell her story, she offers her heart as a guide. Whether she is describing the fog of those early days, the healing she found in community, or the legacy she continues to build for Danny. She reminds us that healing is possible. Although, it wasn't easy. If you find yourself hiding behind grief or simply need a nudge to move forward, you will find her story a game changer.

As you read *Selfish Grief: Redefining Healing After Loss*, I encourage you to lean into your raw emotions. You may cry. You may nod your head in recognition of a similar point or feeling. You may even find yourself journaling your own pain and hope in the margins. Most of all, you will be reminded that you are not alone.

— Rev. Dr. Cathy Wilkins Moffitt, Founder, Heartfelt International Ministries, Inc.

A LETTER TO THE READER

When I first sat down to write these words, I promised myself I would not sugarcoat the journey. Grief is raw, unpredictable, and deeply personal. There is no correct way to grieve, and no perfect timeline for healing.

I wrote this book not as an instruction manual, but as a companion, something to whisper hope when the silence of loss feels unbearable. My deepest prayer is that these pages remind you that *you are not alone.*

In the days after my husband's passing, I often found strength in journaling, in therapy, and in the kindness of others. I encourage you to explore those same tools, or whatever helps you breathe through the weight of your own loss. Healing is work, but it is sacred work.

As you turn each page, may you find courage to take one more step, faith to believe in tomorrow, and hope to know that joy after loss is possible.

"Til God takes the last breath from my body"

DESTINY REALIZED
By Othell J. Miller

Malika to Danny

Long legs toned like steel/eyes romantic as the skies/
Walking with swag amongst a crowd of guys/
Caught my attention and provoked a smile/
Before I looked away like an innocent child/
Content with the joy of a stolen glance/
Clueless that seeds of future romance/
Were set in motion behind the scenes/
For years would pass and fate would bring/
Your light into my world again/
Bearing the gifts of a loyal friend/
You made me laugh you gave your ear/
You really listened so you could hear/
The priceless rhythms of a woman's heart/
With quiet skill you showed the art/
Of chivalry/
Reviving hopes of love from casualty/
It AMAZES me/
Now every time I look at you/
I can say that dreams DO come true/

Danny to Malika

Cocoa skin smooth as silk/smile splendid as the sun/
My eyes were transfixed/my heart was won/
The instant I beheld your face/
I was weakened by your grace/
My mind said pursue/
But my legs stood in place/
Unsure of just what to say/
Feelings unspoken that day/
Yet thoughts of you continued to play/
In my mind/
A wonderful dream untainted by time/
For as the years would come and go/
Visions of you would often flow/
Through prayers and dreams/it seems/
I could not shake this recurring scene/ of
You and I connected in a sweet love story/
And to see it unfold/
I give God the glory
For truly His hand played a role in this/
Divine ceremony of love and bliss/
I'm forever grateful to have the chance/
To partner with you in this glorious dance of life/
Overjoyed to say "MiLane's" my wife/

The New Definition of Selfish

Grief doesn't come with a manual. It barges in, loud and uninvited, rearranging every piece of the life you thought you'd have. Fourteen months after marrying the man I had prayed for, I found myself staring at a life I didn't recognize, one I hadn't planned to walk alone. I was a newlywed and a widow; both titles stitched together by love and abruptly torn apart by loss.

In the early days of my grief, I stumbled through emotions so big that they felt like they would swallow me whole. But amid the fog, one word kept resurfacing: **selfish,** not because I was being called that by others, but because I began to say it and ask myself, Is it selfish to not answer the phone? Is it selfish not to show up to family events? Is it selfish to say "No" when I simply have no more energy to give?

Then I realized something. I wasn't being selfish in the traditional sense. I was being unapologetically selfish, which my mentor had given me permission to do on that dreaded day, and I had to be. The world around me kept spinning, but mine had completely stopped. I had to give myself permission to stop also. To heal, I needed to guard my space fiercely. I needed time to cry, scream, sleep, write, and sit in silence without guilt. I needed to prioritize myself, not to neglect others, but to simply survive.

Grieving redefined selfishness for me. It showed me that taking care of myself mentally, emotionally, and spiritually wasn't just okay. It was NECESSARY. Through setting boundaries, resting when I was weary, forgiving my mistakes, and speaking kindly to myself, I honored God who created me. As I reflect now, I realize He was with me all the way, dropping what I call GOD NUGGETS.

Sometimes, the most radical act of healing is saying, "Right now, I need to choose me!"

A Love Worth the Wait

Let's give it a try.

I first saw Danny while standing in the hallway of Bray Hall. I was a freshman at Lane College, getting my classes, a bit nervous, new to everything, and in came a group of upperclassmen basketball players. Danny stood out . . . tall, confident, and strikingly handsome. He didn't say anything then, but I noticed him. I never could've known that I had just laid eyes on my future husband.

According to a letter he wrote years later, one I hold dear and shared below, he noticed me too. In fact, it was more than noticed; it was instant for him. He saw my smile and told his friends, "Mane, ain't nobody's teeth supposed to be that white!" That was classic Danny, funny and bold, but shy when it came to matters of the heart.

Even though we were always around each other, having the same major, attending the same events, and hanging in the same campus circles, he never told me he was interested. We joked, we laughed, and we supported each other. But dating never happened, not in college. What we didn't know was that a seed had been planted, one that would take 25 years to bloom.

After graduation, life moved us in different directions. I pursued my career path. He raised his daughter. We crossed paths now and then. We even saw each other at homecomings and on social media sites, with short calls here and there, but the friendship remained exactly that, friendship. Still, unbeknownst to me, he never stopped thinking of me. I never knew that when he prayed for someone with a beautiful soul to walk into his life, my name and my face always came to mind.

It wasn't until, January 2012, that he finally called and said the words I never expected: "I have admired you for 25 years, and if you are not currently dating, I would like to court you and see if we have a chance." I was stunned and speechless!

5

I asked him for a little time to think and pray about it, and exactly one week later, he called again. That's when I said the words that changed everything . . . "Let's give it a try." From that moment on, January 13, 2012, we started our journey, one rooted in decades of knowing, admiring, and longing. It wasn't rushed. It was real. It was everything I had prayed for too.

On October 12, 2013, that admiration turned into covenant. I became Mrs. Malika Williams, his wife, his answered prayer, and he was mine.

In Danny's Words: How Our Story Began

"Beautiful!" is the one word that came to mind when I saw Malika Brown. I met Malika when she was an incoming freshman at Lane College in Jackson, TN. I remember being with other basketball players and seeing how she had the most beautiful white smile. I told one of my friends, "Mane, ain't nobody's teeth supposed to be that white!"

My boys, Enarday and Damon, could see I was interested in Malika, and I was hoping at least one of them would let her know because I, for some reason, didn't have the nerve to approach her. Well, needless to say, they didn't tell her. As the years went on, my so-called friends never let her know, I decided maybe I need to get the nerve up to approach her in a romantic manner. I would laugh and joke with her and make small talk, but nerves would always get the best of me.

At the beginning of my junior year at Lane, I said to myself: I've got to let her know how interested I am, since it was painfully obvious that my friends were not letting her know how much I thought of her. I can remember when she became Ms. Lane College, and I said to myself, "She is a perfect Ms. Lane College, and she sure will look good on my arm. I'm gonna get my MiLane!" (Almost everybody from Memphis would call her this. LOL). Junior year ended and still no Malika in my life.

Senior year comes, and I'm thinking this is the last hurrah for me; it's now or never. The year begins with seeing each other on campus, and again, just friendly laughter and conversation. I had come up with a plan that since I played basketball, and I knew she attended games; I would get her to notice me by winking at her during my games. Well, it didn't work as I planned. She just figured this was Danny being Danny.

Years passed and I never stopped thinking about her. I would see her at Lane homecomings over the years, but I still never mentioned how I admired her from the first day I saw her. We continued to stay in touch, either by phone calls or through social media, and the friendship continued to grow.

During this entire time, while raising my daughter, I often asked GOD to place someone with a beautiful soul in our lives. It seems each time I said this prayer; Malika Brown was the name or face I saw. I thought, "Naw, this can't be. Too much time has passed." However, at the beginning of 2012, I said, "GOD, if this is who I'm supposed to be with, order my words in expressing myself to her and please give me the courage to say it!"

I called Malika that evening and was really nervous, but I managed to tell her that for 25 years, I have admired her and thought the world of her, but I did not have the courage to tell her how I felt. She was totally surprised and caught off guard. I told her if she would allow me, I wanted to court her and build this relationship. She asked me for a little time to think about it and call her within a week. I called her exactly a week to the day and she said, "Let's give it a try."

So, since January 13, 2012, we have been giving our LOVE a try, and it has been everything I've wanted and more. On October 12, 2013, my 25-year admiration will become a reality when Malika "MiLane" Brown becomes my soul mate for life.

Danny

Our Wedding Day

At last!

Today was a whirlwind of perfect emotions that I'll never forget. The morning began with nervous laughter, a thousand butterflies, and a thunderstorm pounding over Memphis. Sheets of rain soaked the outdoor space we'd reserved so carefully, but even with soaked chairs and puddles on the brick, I held onto peace . . . thanks in part to my sister-friend, Vanessa, who arrived early with warm coffee, a calm spirit, and unwavering reassurance. She had been my anchor through most of the planning.

The beauty team circled in like angels, curling and pinning and making me laugh through a few nervous tears. My hairdresser, Thea cracked jokes and dabbed my cheeks as she worked, and together, we kept the joyful emotions in check.

Then, just one hour before the ceremony, the rain stopped. The clouds cleared as if Heaven itself had peeled them away, and the sun came out, bold, bright, and unapologetically radiant.

When "At Last" by Etta James began to play, I stepped into that aisle, the sunlight dancing on my skin. I felt like I was walking into a dream. I looked ahead, and there he was, My Danny, My answered prayer! Tears welled in his eyes, and that was all I needed to see. My heart found home in his gaze, and every ounce of stress melted away.

The vows were everything, personal, flirtatious, and tender. We promised things no one else heard; only we needed to understand. I remember the way his hand trembled slightly as he held mine, and the soft gasp I heard from the crowd as he said, "You are my forever." There were a few misty eyes in the seats. Some of his buddies even had to clear their throats and look away. That made us laugh quietly during the prayer.

The reception was a blur of music, dancing, speeches, and joy. My maid of honor and matron of honor, powerhouses of humor and heart, gave toasts that turned the entire room into a mix of tear-streaked cheeks and deep belly laughs. The flowers were perfect. The cake was rich. The love in the air was undeniable.

In the stillness of our honeymoon suite, the music has faded. The guests have gone home, and it's just us, me and this incredible man I get to call my husband. We're tired. We're blissful. We're holding the joy like a soft secret we want to keep forever.

Now, hours later, I sit in silence. My wedding dress is carefully draped over a chair; its lace and satin holding the energy of the day. My bouquet rests beside it, still fragrant, still glowing. I'm trying to take it all in . . . because it really happened. I'm married! I am Mrs. Malika Williams!

Tomorrow, we begin our life together. But tonight, I'm holding onto the bliss, just a little while longer.

Our First and Only Anniversary

Our First and Only Year of Forever

It was our first and only year of marriage. Danny passed exactly fourteen months to the day we said, "I do." Looking back now, I hold that year as a sacred treasure, a gift wrapped in laughter, learning, and love. It was a year that taught me not only how to be a wife, but how to lean into God's grace as He wove two lives into one.

Our first year of marriage was blissful, though not without its adjustments. For me, it meant leaving Nashville and relocating to Lee's Summit, Missouri. Suddenly, I was waking up to blankets of snow, sometimes eight inches or more at a time. For this Tennessee girl, it was an entirely new world. But my sweet husband, ever attentive, made sure I was cared for. He took me shopping for real winter clothes, no more "cute" coats that couldn't stand a chance against Missouri's icy winds. He rearranged the garage, so I could park my car inside. He even taught me how to shovel snow. What could have felt burdensome became joyful because Danny had a way of making everything an adventure.

Danny and his daughter welcomed me with open arms. Becoming a "bonus mom" was both an adjustment and an honor. I showed up at games, planned birthday sleepovers and prom nights, learned the rhythms of teenage life, and I embraced the role with joy. Of course, like any couple, Danny and I had to navigate the small frictions of learning one another's habits—how we kept the house, how we organized life, and how we each functioned best. But with clear communication, God's guidance, and our unshakable love, even the smallest conflicts only strengthened us.

That year was also marked by milestones. Danny received a promotion, and together, we dreamed of relocating to Dallas within the year. His daughter was accepted to the University of Pine Bluff Arkansas, and we had the joy of helping her prepare, pack and plan a fun road trip to Arkansas to help her get settled into her next exciting season. We laughed all the way as we moved her things into her dorm, and Danny stayed strong until the moment we drove off campus; then the tears finally came. It was a glimpse into the depth of his love as both a father and a man.

And then came our first wedding anniversary. It was simple, beautiful, and perfect. We didn't need grandeur because the gift was in being together. We went out for a fabulous dinner, shared stories, and laughed like newlyweds do. Danny had a way of looking at me that made me feel like the most cherished woman in the world. That night, as we reflected on our first year, we talked about our dreams for Dallas, about the home we hoped to build, and about the life we were certain we'd share for years to come.

We didn't know then that it would be the only anniversary we'd celebrate together. But oh, what a gift it was. Our first year of forever taught me that love, when rooted in faith, can fill a lifetime, even when that lifetime is only fourteen months long. That year became a tender foundation, one I would lean on when everything changed, and one that quietly carried me into the chapters that followed.

The Night Before Goodbye

I love you, Lik!

There was nothing unusual about that night. Nothing to hint at how sacred it would become. I moved through my evening routine just as I always did, laying out Danny's clothes for work the next day . . . the navy suit, the crisp shirt, and the tie he'd eventually choose, after playfully debating two or three options.

I made sure his shoes were polished, socks matched, and everything was just so. Some would say I spoiled him, and they'd be right, but I did it with joy. I loved caring for him; it felt like a true privilege. I just simply added to what he already had, a quiet flair when it came to dressing. He loved playing with colors and patterns, matching his shirt and tie like a true artist. I always admired that about him, and a thousand other things.

When we finally got in bed, it was our normal rhythm . . . three kisses, always three. Then, we clasped hands, as we did every night, and began to pray, but something shifted inside me as he prayed. I was overcome with a deep, unshakable wave of gratitude, the kind that pulls from the core of your soul and the kind that makes your voice tremble, and your breath catch.

"Lord, I thank You for my husband," I said repeatedly. The words came out between sobs I couldn't control. I cried so hard; it startled even me. Although startled, it was a quiet weep beneath the stream, thinking about how full my life felt with him in it.

Danny held me tighter. He kissed my forehead and gently whispered, "Lik (his nickname for me), I had this same gratitude cry earlier while I was in the shower." I love you, Lik," he said, with his voice soft, but certain. He wiped my tears, pulled me into his arms, and wrapped me in a peace I had never known before.

We drifted off to sleep that night, still holding hands. It was the best night's sleep I'd had in a long time. I didn't know then . . . it would be our last.

07:55

December 12, 2014

 MESSAGES   Now

Here..have a wonderful day..love you..

Ok love you more

(1/2) Thanks for taking care of me..started raining hard just as i got downtown but i was able to watch them other ninjas get wet as i walked under my Michael

Ok ok!! You are so welcome babe. I love taking care of you! Muah!

(2/2) Korz umbrella:)

The Train to Eternity

Good morning, Gorgeous!

Those were the first words Danny whispered to me on the morning of
December 12, 2014. He sweetly asked, *"Are you taking me to the train
station this morning?"* Still half asleep, I smiled and mumbled, "Yes."

Through my sleep-hazed vision, I saw the smile that had
brightened my days for the past 14 months. His joy was radiant and
familiar. *"Great!"* he said, and his tone made my heart feel full. You see,
my husband loved it when I took him to the train station. It was our
sacred time of morning conversations, warm coffee, laughter, and the
ritual of listening to the daily prank calls on the radio. It was our
rhythm, our way of starting the day connected.

That morning was no different. We were both excited, counting
down the hours. After work, we'd begin our holiday break, heading
back home to Tennessee to see family and breathe in the warmth of the
holiday season.

We said our usual goodbyes with three kisses—always three.
That was Danny's rule: "One for the Father, one for the Son, and one
for the Holy Ghost," he'd say with a wink.

I watched him buy his train ticket at the kiosk. He turned to
wave, with that huge, goofy smile on his face, and then he disappeared
into the crowd like he always did. About 20 minutes later, my phone
buzzed with a text from him, our little ritual. "Here..have a wonderful
day..love you..Thanks for taking care of me..started raining hard just as
I got downtown, but I was able to watch them other ninjas get wet as I
walked under my Michael Kors umbrella that my baby just bought me,
always covering me." Again, that was classic Danny, making me laugh
and making sure I knew how much he appreciated me.

The rest of the day moved quickly . . . dry cleaners, last-minute
gifts, and prepping for our trip. I had a 2:00 p.m. appointment with
Ungie, the magician behind my hair, at Khimandi Hair Studio in

Arlington, TX. The visit was smooth and full of laughter and light talk. By late afternoon, I was back home . . . hair flawless and a full heart. I made myself a quick snack and stretched out across the bed carefully, of course. Ladies, you know we don't mess up a fresh hairdo. Just before I laid down, I got a text from Danny: "Hey, Lik! I'll be on the 4:40 p.m. train. Can't wait to see you and grab your booty."

I laughed out loud and replied, "You are so fresh, but I love it." Even now, I can still hear his voice when I read those words, playful, loving, and mine.

Although I didn't feel tired, sleep came over me like a heavy blanket, the kind of sleep you don't see coming. I drifted off, deeper than I expected, and when I opened my eyes again, the clock stared back at me, and panic set in . . . I overslept! I quickly grabbed my phone and texted, "I overslept, Babe, but I'm on my way! I'm running out the door!" There was no response. That was strange. Danny always texted right back. I assumed he might still be on the train, where spotty signal service wasn't uncommon, and I tried not to let my anxiety rise.

When I arrived at the station, I looked around, expecting to see Danny standing there with that signature smile, lighting up the sidewalk. There was no one. The platform was quiet. Still, I texted again, and nothing. Something in me stirred. It was a low hum of unease. I sat there, watching the minutes tick by as the silence grew louder.

As I waited, I called my closest circle, two of my besties, Alainna and my prayer partner, Tamida. I didn't want to panic, but I needed someone to know. I needed to say out loud that something wasn't right because deep in my spirit . . . I already knew.

Sometimes the search for a loved one becomes a spiritual chorus, one voice after another rising in harmony, in panic, in prayer, until truth is revealed.

Finding Danny: A Chorus of Concern
Written by My Best Friend, Alainna Stephens

"I remember the day with such vivid details. My best friend, Malika, who had recently moved from Tennessee to Texas, and I were on the phone having one of our usual, lighthearted conversations. She was in the car, heading to pick up her Danny from the train station. As always, we laughed about this and that, just enjoying the ease of our friendship.

She mentioned she had pulled up to the stop and was waiting for his train to arrive. A few moments later, she said another call was coming in and clicked over. When she returned, her tone had shifted. She explained that she had received a call telling her she needed to come to the downtown Dallas Baylor Hospital. There were no details and no explanation. My heart sank. I couldn't understand how such news could come without clarity, and I could only imagine her confusion matching my own.

I urged her to call a local friend to meet her at the hospital, not knowing what awaited her there. As for me, I continued with my day, but my spirit remained heavy. I prayed silently, asking God to cover her, to protect her husband, Dannyboy, and to give us all strength.

That evening, I drew a bath, hoping to quiet my racing mind. I didn't want to overwhelm Malika with my own questions or emotions, so I chose to wait, trusting God and keeping her lifted in prayer. Then the phone rang. It was Sherrie, Malika's sister. On the other end, all I could hear was muffled words through uncontrollable sobs. I asked her to calm down, so I could understand. Then, through her broken voice, I heard the words clearly: "He's gone. Danny is gone."

I froze. My phone slipped into the side of the bathtub as I sat in stunned silence. A wave of grief poured out of me, with tears flowing, not only for my own heartbreak, but for the deep, unimaginable pain I knew my best friend was enduring. The distance between us felt unbearable at that moment. All I wanted was to be by her side . . . to hold her and to support her.

Malika called me soon after. We wept together. I didn't want to intrude on her family's time, so I asked gently if she wanted me there. Her answer was

immediate: "Please come." That was all I needed to hear. By the next morning, I was on the first plane I could find.

Time seemed to stop. Everything else could wait. My heart was broken for her, but I knew my role now was simple, yet sacred. Show up. Be present. Let God guide me in giving her the comfort, strength, and companionship she needed as she stepped into this painful new chapter of her life.

Alainna

Finding Danny: A Chorus of Concern
Written by My Prayer Warrior Bestie, Tamida Brockington

"*It was a beautiful end to a busy work week. The weather was calm, the sun was shining, and the rest that the weekend provided was upon us. Ride home check-ins were a common thing, rehashing the day, the busy week, sharing giggles about marriage and the new discoveries it brings.*

We sat on the phone for about fifteen minutes waiting for Danny to emerge from the train station. After about thirty minutes, and still no Danny, Malika decided to hang up and go inside and look around . . . still not finding anything too strange about his, not bouncing out of the station with excitement to see her waiting for him. After a few moments, my phone rang again and to my surprise, Danny was not with Malika.

The weight of the concern started to build especially because he hadn't rung her phone to let you know he was running a little late or that he was tied up. Something wasn't right!

As we were trying to figure out where Danny could be, there was a beep on her phone. It was Baylor Hospital calling. We ended our call briefly. A few moments felt like a few hours, as I pulled into the garage of our home. The next few moments would change the trajectory of her life forever."

Tamida

Finding Danny: A Chorus of Concern

The Call No Wife Should Take – Baylor University Medical Center

Me: Hello?

Caller: Is this Mrs. Malika Williams?

Me: It is!

Caller: This is the nurse at Baylor University Medical Center. Your husband, Danny, has had an accident, and we need you to get to Baylor on Gaston Avenue as safely and as quickly as possible.

Me: Jesus! What? Is he alive?

Caller: I'm sorry. We cannot give that type of information over the phone. Once you arrive, pull under the emergency room overhang and call this number. One of our staff members will come out and lead you in.

Me: Jesus, help! Thank you, I'm on my way.

My Frantic Call to Tamida

"Mida, Danny had an accident. I am headed to the hospital. Please call Vanessa and pray." My heart was pounding so hard against my chest, I could see the movement through my shirt.

Adding to the Chorus
Written by Tamida Brockington

"I not only called Vanessa, but another prayer warrior and good friend, because I knew this called for deep intercession. As we began to pray for Danny, I had a sense that our prayers should shift to Malika. It was so heavy.

With tears flowing and hearts united, we bombarded heaven on Malika's behalf. We prayed for God's peace and His strength to bring her through whatever was on the other side of uncertainty. We prayed and believed God that HIS will would be done and would be well."

Tamida

Finding Danny: A Chorus of Concern
My Assigned Angel

Just as I was hanging up with the nurse, my mentor, Cathy called.

Me: Hello?

Cathy: Maliiiiikkkkkaaaaa, with her strong southern drawl, where are you?

Me: I'm at the train station, and I can't find Danny!!! *"I'm on my way to get you, the hospital called me as well, because I am the emergency contact for you and Danny that they found in his wallet. Denise and I are on the way. The traffic is terrible, so we will be there as soon as we can."*

Me: Okay. Thank you so much.

As I waited for Cathy and Denise to arrive, I remember asking God to equip me to take care of my "Sweet Baby," whatever his condition may be. I then decided to walk the empty train station lot to try and calm myself down. As I walked, I began to worship singing, "The Anthem" by Todd Dulaney. You see . . . the Sunday before this dreaded day, Danny and I attended church, and the choir sang this song. He fell in love with it and hummed it the rest of the day, asking me who the artist was and would I add it to his playlist.

Shortly after my walk, Cathy and Denise arrived. I jumped in the truck and off to Baylor Hospital we went. The traffic was horrific. It seemed as if we caught every light and traffic delay we could. I remember the ride being eerily quiet, as my stomach continued to rumble, and nausea began to take over.

Cathy decided to call her doctor friend to see if she could call the hospital to get more details. She placed the call, and within minutes the doctor called back. Cathy answered the call on speaker phone and the doctor asked, *"Am I on speaker phone?"*

Cathy: Yes, the doctor replied, "Take me off!"

I could tell by the authoritative tone and firmness in her voice, that it was not good. Cathy's only words were, *"Okay. I understand,"* and she ended the call.

We arrived at the hospital, and I called the number the nurse provided. The nurse answered and said, *"We are on the way."* I remember entering the emergency waiting room, and it felt so heavy, like everyone was staring at me.

Light Switch

Who is Mrs. Williams?

In the emergency room, I was met by a chaplain. Her voice was kind but measured, as though she was trying to hold something heavy in her hands without letting it fall. I was led to a small waiting area where I briefly sat down. After only a few moments, she asked, *"Do you feel like you're able to stand and walk?"*

"Yes," I replied, though something in me was already unraveling. *"Okay,"* she said gently. *"Come with me, and we'll go into a room where you can speak with the physician."*

My mentor, the chaplain, and I walked slowly down the sterile hallway to a quiet room. The lights were bright, and the air was cold. We took our seats, and I remember thinking, *I just want to see my husband.*

Moments later, a physician walked in. He greeted us calmly and then looked around the room. *"Who is Mrs. Williams?"* he asked. I lifted my hand and answered softly, but with pride, "I am." He sat down across from me, introduced himself, and said the words that would change my life forever. *"Your husband had an accident this afternoon."*

I leaned forward. "Okay," I said cautiously, bracing myself.

"Was your husband on any medication?" he asked.
"He was on a very small dosage of blood pressure medicine," I replied. "He recently had his physical and it was all positive. He was doing well."

The doctor nodded slightly. *"Your husband had an accident,"* he repeated, *"and he did not survive."* Those last three words, *"did not survive,"* echoed in my mind louder than any sound I had ever heard. They didn't make sense. I heard them, but I couldn't understand them. I was suspended in time, waiting for the world to correct itself. The doctor continued, almost searching for a way to soften the blow. Finally, he said, *"It's as if someone turned his light switch off."* That was the moment, the exact moment my soul splintered.

I sat there in that cold, bright hospital room, where just seconds ago I was a wife, waiting to greet her husband. Now, I was a widow who was fighting for breath, struck by a grief that knocked the wind out of me. I whispered, "What?" even though I'd already heard him. The same breathless awe I had every time I looked at Danny's handsome face was now matched by a crushing pain that wrapped around my chest. I was suffocating in disbelief. I repeated it out loud . . . "I don't understand!"

We, the chaplain and I, slowly walked toward the sliding door. She kept her steady hand on my shoulder, while my sweet mentor, Cathy, was holding my hand and whispering prayers as we moved.

When the sheet was pulled back, I saw him, my "Sweet Baby." His face was so beautiful, so peaceful, and so still. In that moment, I knew that a large part of me died, too. The pain wasn't just emotional; it was physical. It felt like supernatural surgery was taking place inside of me, right there on the floor of that hospital. I couldn't move. I couldn't cry. I could only feel the silence surrounding me, but everything was loud, my heartbeat, the humming lights, and the echo of finality. The room dimmed around me. I remember thinking, *"Am I passing out?* It wasn't just shock. It was grief fog, thick as the San Francisco Bay fog and just as unrelenting. I would live inside that dense fog for three long years.

I asked to go to the restroom because I felt like I was going to throw up. My mentor came with me. We paused in the bathroom, and I held the sink, trying to catch my breath. My soul was crying louder than my body could. Cathy looked at me with tears in her eyes and said something I'll never forget: *"I'm so, so sorry, Little Sis,"* she whispered. *"This is bigger than you, and as you begin this healing journey, this is your time to be unapologetically SELFISH!"* I didn't understand those words at the time, but I nodded, holding onto her voice like a rope in the storm.

We returned to the room, and I asked if I could have my husband's belongings. I turned to the doctor and thanked him sincerely.

"If you need to leave," I said, "I understand. I know there are people in this hospital who need you far more than I do."

He looked at me with sadness in his eyes and said, *"No. I'm going to sit here with you for a while. This one has deeply bothered me. To see a young, 47-year-old man in great shape and so full of life consumed by a heart attack . . . this is really tough for me."* So, we sat. It was a grieving wife, a caring doctor, a shattered mentor, and the echo of a light switch being flipped, leaving everything in the dark.

The Closet

After what felt like hours wrapped in sterile silence and heartbreak, it was time to leave the hospital. I didn't want to go. Part of me hoped that if I stayed long enough, someone would walk in and tell me they were wrong. There had been a mistake, and my husband, my love, my life, my Danny, was still alive. That moment never came.

As we made our way toward the exit, my mentor and other friends gently pleaded with me to come home with them. They wanted to keep me close, wrapped in love and support, and I understood. I couldn't! I needed to go home to the space that Danny and I built together . . . to the rooms still filled with his laughter, to the bed still holding his warmth, and to the air still scented by his cologne. I needed to be surrounded by him. It was the only way I could breathe. They didn't understand at first, but they respected my wishes.

When we pulled up to our home, I sat in the car for a long moment, staring at the door. That familiar brick exterior had always represented comfort, joy, and love, but now, as I stepped inside, a cold emptiness met me like a wall. He wasn't there to greet me, no hug and no "Hey, Lik." That's when the truth finally hit.

The void was instant and overwhelming. I dropped my bags and ran to our bedroom. I walked into our closet and collapsed, right onto his shoes and his clothes, breathing in the last traces of his scent; they were my oxygen. There, I wept like I had never wept before. It wasn't just from grief, but from a soul-deep ache that left my body trembling. The sound that came out of me wasn't a cry; it was a wail, a guttural, unfiltered mourning that I had no control over.

I clung to the fabric of his shirts, pressing my face into the folds, as if doing so would call him back. This is where I stayed, curled up in a closet of memories and surrounded by the remnants of the man I loved. I couldn't move. I didn't want to move. If I stayed in that closet, maybe I could pause time. Maybe I could hold onto the illusion that Danny was just in the other room, or that he would walk in and find me crying and scoop me up the way he always did. That night passed in blurred hours . . . no sleep; it was just grief and silence.

Early the next morning, I heard a knock at the door. It was my mother, my sister, and two of my dearest friends. They had taken the first flights from Tennessee and Atlanta, moving heaven and earth to get to me. Their presence felt like sunlight breaking through the thick, choking fog. They didn't try to fix me; they just showed up and began the sacred work of helping me put the shattered pieces of my life back together.

Even with their arms around me, I felt . . . LOST. Danny's passing didn't just make me a widow. It made me feel like an invalid, hollowed out. It felt like my identity had been stripped away in a single moment.

I was so proud to be his wife. To be honest, I must say right now: Being the best wife I could be was one of my deepest desires. I poured myself into our love, into our home, and into every detail of our lives together. And now, all of it, everything I had dreamed of, planned for, and prayed for was gone. I was no longer Mrs. Williams in the way I had been just hours before, but in my heart, I still was and always would be.

Although our marriage was brief, just fourteen months, it was more than many people experience in a lifetime. Those days and those moments were sacred. They were rich with laughter, deep conversation, unwavering encouragement, and a peace that I had only imagined. Just being in Danny's presence brought me a sense of fullness that words can barely contain. We did so much in that short time. We traveled. We established a home filled with joy and mutual respect. We helped guide his daughter into her next chapter, taking her to college and getting her settled. We shared everyday routines and extraordinary dreams. We celebrated life together, one beautiful day at a time.

People would ask us all the time, "How long have you two been married?" When we would answer, "A little over a year," the shock was almost always the same. "No way," they would say. "Y'all you've been together forever."

In a way, we had. It felt like our souls had known each other long before we reconnected. We were two people who had finally been aligned by divine timing. Danny would often say, "When God connects you with the right person, everything just works." And it did. It flowed. We flowed.

The beauty of our bond wasn't just in the grand gestures, but in the small things. There were the inside jokes, the late-night talks, and the quiet understanding that didn't need words. Those fourteen months taught me what it meant to be fully seen, loved, and covered by someone who was truly my partner in every sense.

Even though the chapter of our marriage ended far too soon, the story of our love continues to live on in my heart, in the lessons I carry, and in every person who witnessed our wedding and the light we shared.

And so, in the words of my dear childhood friend Simone, who witnessed it all unfold, here is how she remembers the light, the love, and the beauty of our wedding.

Witnessed Light by Simone Ghoston-Brown

"Your wedding was one of the most beautiful I've ever attended, and not just because of the stunning décor or the vibrant colors; though, those were lovely. What made it truly unforgettable was the overwhelming sense of love that filled the space.

The way you and Danny looked at each other and the way you moved through that day as one was palpable. I could see it. I could feel it, and that's not something you experience at every wedding. It was extraordinary.

Now that Danny is no longer with us, I understand even more deeply why I was so moved that day. The love you shared radiated through every moment. I remember thinking, "Malika is so happy." I didn't just witness your love; I felt it. As a guest, I felt seen, appreciated, and wrapped in that love too. That's a rare gift, and I'll never forget it.

Simone

JOURNAL ENTRY

There's an indescribable ache
deep in my heart...
a quiet emptiness
that words can't quite hold...
a void
that reminds me
something is missing.

The Days That Followed

The days immediately following Danny's passing felt like being suspended in fog, thick, gray, and heavy. I moved through it, not with clarity, not with energy, but only with necessity. There were things that had to be done, calls to make, an apartment to pack, and a life to uproot. I was still breathing, but nothing about it felt natural. Everything was forced and mechanical. Grief has a way of slowing down time while speeding up the world around you.

In the middle of that aching stillness, God sent help, tender and steady help. The Williams family, my in-laws, stepped in with such compassion and grace that I still weep today when I think of it. My mother-in-love, all of my sisters-in-love, and my nieces and nephews, reached out to me in the gentlest way, not with demands or expectations, but with love. They told me they would take care of everything regarding the service, planning it, organizing the details, and writing the obituary. They lived in Memphis, so the logistics made sense, but the spirit in which they did it was something else entirely.

They didn't move without me. They included me in every conversation, every decision, and asking for my input and final approval, as if I were the most honored person in the room. They certainly didn't have to do that; they could have done it differently. I've heard horror stories from other widows about how quickly their in-laws became distant or even adversarial, but not the Williams family. God chose them for me, and for that, I am endlessly grateful.

They held me in that season, in such a tender, loving, and gentle way, which made a permanent imprint on my soul. Even now, they still carry me in that same spirit of love. It is not just a blessing. It is a legacy.

Before, During, and the Aftershock

Now I say . . . Sleep well in the arms of Jesus, my Beloved Dannyboy.

I remember the day I flew from Texas back to Tennessee with my mom, my best friend, Alainna, and our beloved dog, Mocha. Just days before, this same group of women surrounded me as I wept over Danny's shoes in our bedroom closet. Now, they were carrying me again, but this time, it was toward the unthinkable—my husband's funeral.

Alainna's dear friend, Marsha, offered to drive us to the airport. This woman, whom I barely knew at the time, had already been so gracious by bringing food, supplies, and comfort to our apartment in the immediate aftermath of Danny's passing—along with others who sent flowers, food and so much more. Marsha's kindness felt holy, and her presence was steady in a way I needed. When we arrived at the airport, I grabbed my suitcase and Mocha's carrier, and Marsha gently took my hand, pulled me into a hug, and whispered, "You've got this. You are stronger than this." I hear those words even now, years later. In moments when my chest gets tight or my heart gets heavy, I hear her voice. God had tucked another angel into the folds of my grief.

The flight from Texas to Tennessee was the longest I've ever taken, even though I've flown the route dozens of times. That day, every second was weighty. I sat there in disbelief, knowing I was returning to Tennessee . . . not for the holidays with my husband as planned, but to bury him.

When we landed, another angel awaited me. My longtime hairstylist, Thea Jones, who had styled my hair on my wedding day, met me at the airport and immediately offered to take me to her shop, although it was not regular business hours. She wanted to help me feel like myself, even if just for a few hours, before the hardest day of my life. She shampooed, conditioned, and styled my hair with tenderness, and we sat together quietly, no pressure for conversation, just presence. It was a kindness I didn't know I needed.

The next day, we drove to Memphis for the funeral. My mother, sister and I stayed with my cousins the night before. Their home was warm and welcoming, filled with the buzz of preparation and children's laughter. I tried to participate, and I tried to smile and engage, but I was quiet, wrapped in layers of disbelief. How was I preparing to bury the man I had only just married, the man I planned to grow old with? That night, I barely slept.

When morning came, I stepped into the shower, hoping it would bring some calm, but it was at that moment that I broke. My grief rose like a wave and knocked me off my feet. I sobbed so hard that my knees buckled, and I had to sit on the edge of the tub while the water poured over me. I was engulfed with the kind of crying that empties you . . . the kind you never forget. Eventually, I gathered enough strength to get dressed.

We were late for the funeral because of my breakdown, but the Williams family didn't make me feel rushed or guilty. They were patient, gentle, and full of grace.

When we arrived at the church, I was stunned by what I saw. There were crowds of people, outside and inside, standing shoulder to shoulder, and wall to wall. There were classmates from college, Danny's friends from high school and middle school, his fraternity brothers, my sorority sisters, and friends and family from California and across the country. All were there for Danny! All were there for us!

As I climbed the church steps, the first person I saw was my father. He hugged me tightly and said, "If it gets to be too much, step out. I'll be right out here waiting." Just his voice gave me a little strength.

Then I walked down the aisle. There he was. Seeing Danny's body took me straight back to the hospital, back to that sterile, cold room where the light switch of my life had been turned off. My legs trembled. I felt like I might collapse, but something locked within me. Some force, maybe grace, maybe God, maybe both, held me upright. I stood still. I stared. How could this be?

I took my seat between my mother and my sister. The obituary rested on my lap like a stone. My eyes dropped to the floor. Tears slid quietly down my cheeks and soaked into my dress. I sat like that until it was time, time for me to speak and to share words at his family's request, the words I never wanted to say, but somehow, I did.

I remember approaching the pulpit, my sister by my side; her hand was like an anchor holding me steady in a sea of grief. I stood before a sanctuary full of faces, some familiar and some not, but I couldn't see them clearly. The room felt both silent and thunderously loud. The air was thick, but I couldn't feel it.

Until We Meet Again . . .

It is with deep appreciation that I stand before you to say, "Thank you all" for being so supportive of me during this tragic and difficult time. Many have expressed how my beloved Danny was so happy as my husband and guess what, he made me equally happy. I am an extremely blessed lady to have been hand-picked by God to be joined to this amazingly witty, loving, and phenomenal man. And while it was only a short 14 months of marital bliss, it is a true love that so many have yet to experience. To the Williams family, I am filled with gratitude that you accepted me as one of your own, and you will eternally be a part of those whom I consider family.

People have since told me that my words were moving. What I shared was heartfelt, beautiful, and powerful. Truthfully, I don't remember any of it, not a single sentence. I believe I spoke through a haze, a protective veil cast over me by God or grief or both, just so I could survive.

When I turned to leave the pulpit, my eyes fell on the casket in front of me . . . My Danny! My Sweet Baby! There was this amazing man who made me laugh every morning, who kissed me three times before every goodbye, and who couldn't wait to "grab my booty" after work. Now, here he was . . . Still. Silent. Gone.

My heart sank so deeply that I thought it might never come back again. My sister squeezed my hand tighter as we walked back to our seats. I sat down, and from that moment forward, the rest of the service became a blur. It was like something in me went to sleep, a deep, inward sleep. It was not to escape the pain, but to survive it. I believe it was a form of divine mercy, shielding me from the full weight of the moment. I don't remember... I don't remember the eulogy. I don't remember who spoke. I don't remember who hugged me. I don't remember the music or the words or the tears around me.

I do have a faint memory of the repass. I remember it feeling peaceful, pleasant, and even like a warm hug from the village that had wrapped itself around me, but even that is foggy. What I remember most is the quiet thankfulness in my soul that somehow, I got through it, and that somehow, the day did not swallow me whole. It's in moments like this you learn something about yourself you never wanted to know. You are stronger than you ever imagined, not because you want to be and not because you're trying to prove anything, but because grief doesn't give you a choice.

With the funeral services behind me, and the support of friends and family, it was time to shift my energy to another massive undertaking . . . packing up our apartment in Texas, the place Danny and I had shared. Every drawer, every photo frame, and every pair of shoes whispered memories of our love. It was emotional labor that I couldn't have managed on my own, and thank God, I did not have to. Before I could even think about getting boxes and packing, once again, I got a call from two friends. One flew in from California, and the other, who had come the day after I got the news, returned to help. Even in my shattered state, God continued to orchestrate my restoration.

And then there is Peter Griffin . . . My sweet nephew Peter flew from California to Texas, just to help me finalize the packing and drive me from Dallas back to Nashville. I will never forget that gift, not just the physical help, though that was immeasurable, but his presence. Having someone from Danny's bloodline by my side, handling our belongings with care and helping to close one chapter, so I could survive long enough to start another, that was love in action. That was family.

I will forever be indebted to Peter and to the entire Williams family. Because of them, I didn't feel abandoned. I didn't feel forgotten. I felt covered. I felt seen. Even in the hollow spaces left behind by loss, I felt held.

The Silence after the Storm

No, we don't always call. We can't.

Grief doesn't just take your loved one; it sometimes takes your friendships too. In the early days of loss, I thought the people closest to me, some of my family and my longtime friends, whom I called sisters, would be by my side every step of the way. I imagined constant check-ins, a steady stream of support, and the kind of presence that doesn't waver. But grief has a way of revealing the unexpected: Some of the very people I thought I could count on disappeared. It was slow at first; then, it was almost completely. The calls stopped. The texts faded. The silence spoke louder than any words.

At first, I couldn't understand it. Had I done something wrong? Time taught me this truth: It usually isn't malice. It's uncomfortable. People don't know what to do with grief. They don't know what to say, so they say nothing. They don't know how to show up, so they don't. Instead of leaning in, they retreat, telling themselves, "If she needs me, she'll call."

Here's what many don't realize. When you're grieving, you don't even know how to ask for help. You don't know what you need. Some days you can barely lift your head off the pillow. Some days breathing, itself, feels like labor. So, "No, we don't always call. We can't."

This is where another facet of grief begins, the grief of lost friendships, broken family ties, and relationships that were once unshakable, now, never return to what they were. To this day, some of those bonds remain cordial, polite, and surface level. However, they are no longer what they once were. This unfortunately, is another layer of loss you have to process.

If you are walking alongside someone who is grieving, let me tell you this: JUST SHOW UP. Don't worry about saying the perfect thing. Don't worry about being in the way. Call anyway. Text anyway.

Sit in the silence, if you must. If all you can say is, "I don't know what to say, but I'm here," that's enough. PRESENCE IS MORE POWERFUL THAN PERFECTION.

If you are the one grieving, I want you to know that GOD WILL NOT LEAVE YOU ALONE. He will raise up the people you need, even if they don't come from where you expect. For me, He sent women who knew my pain, the "Winning Widows," a sisterhood I never saw coming, but one I thank God for daily.

When people fade, don't mistake their silence as God's. He is still speaking, still sending, and still surrounding you in ways you can't see yet. You may feel like God is subtracting, but if you stay the course and let the hurt, hurt the healing will come, and so will the right people. You are not alone. You will not stay alone. You will make it through.

JOURNAL ENTRY

I cannot believe
it has been 10 months
since you gained your wings...
and today
is also our
two-year wedding anniversary.
How does one cope
with what used to be
and what will never come to pass?
Happy Anniversary,
Sweet Baby.

Two Realities of Grief

When we think about grief, most of us only name the obvious one, the grief of losing the person we love, the one who held our hands, shared our secrets, built our dreams, or even just gave us comfort in their presence. That grief is raw, undeniable, and often the first tidal wave that crashes over us.

Oh, but there is another reality of grief, one that lingers longer, one that sneaks into the quiet moments, one that can sometimes feel heavier than the first. The grief of all the things that will never be, the dreams we built in our heads and hearts, the plans penciled into calendars that never came to pass, and the conversations about "someday" that will never make it to reality. This is the grief of what could have been. And, let me tell you the truth, it is real, it is raw, and it must be processed. If we don't allow ourselves to release those dreams into God's hands, they begin to weigh us down. They anchor us in a past that cannot be revived, while the future God has for us waits just beyond the horizon.

I've often said that grief can feel like a blanket. It's warm, it's familiar, and sometimes, it even feels safe. Although we may hate it, we can find ourselves curling back into it because it's all we know. Here's the risk: If we cling too tightly to the dreams that died with our loved one, we prolong what God wants to resurrect in us.

Yes, grieve the person, grieve the life you thought you would have together. Funeralize the plans, the promises, and the "what could have been." Lay them to rest with the same reverence you did when you said goodbye to your loved one. Then, when you're ready, begin to dream again. Dream with tears in your eyes, if you must. Dream with shaky hands. Dream with the memory of your loved one still guiding your heart. Never stop dreaming, because when you stop dreaming, you stop living. Your healing depends on your choosing life.

The two realities of grief are heavy. If you walk through them honestly, both the loss of the person and the loss of the dreams, you will discover that God has a way of breathing new life into the ashes. He has a way of writing new dreams that don't erase the old ones but honor them as steppingstones to what's next. So, don't stop dreaming, even when it feels impossible or unfair. Keep dreaming, because it is truly a matter of life and death.

JOURNAL ENTRY

Journaling became cathartic for me...
my escape.
Widowhood makes you guarded,
aware,
wiser,
perceptive,
Reflective,
compassionate.
Words fail to paint
an adequate picture of my loss.
Thank you, Danny,
for loving me
COMPLETELY.

When the Silence Settles

There's something no one can truly prepare you for after a great loss, the silence. Once the services are over, the casseroles stop coming, and the house quiets, you are left alone with the silence. And in that silence, the weight of loss becomes even heavier. It seeps into everything, the air, the walls, and the stillness of the night. The silence doesn't shout. It whispers. It lingers. It reminds me.

After the funeral, there were a few back-and-forth trips between Nashville and Texas. I needed to finalize things with Danny's employer and tie up the ends of our life there. The first trip back to Texas was especially hard. It wasn't for closure. It was for duty.

I had to clean out Danny's office. I still remember the way my breath caught when I walked in and saw his things, exactly where he left them, his favorite pens, his coffee cup, our wedding photo, and files. The quiet in that space felt sacred and cruel. Danny loved his job, and he loved his colleagues. They were so gracious and kind, especially Pam Fletcher and Demetrius Jenkins, two Human Resource professionals who became, in that season, unexpected shepherds through a forest of paperwork. They helped me sort, sign, process, and finalize the required paperwork, compassionately walking me through every form and conversation.

The technical demands of widowhood are something no one tells you. While one half of your soul is grieving, the other half is being dragged into responsibility. There's no waiting period, not even a grace window. You're balancing two worlds . . . closing a life chapter while trying to figure out how to keep breathing on your own. It was a painful tug-of-war, one side of me mourning and the other side functioning. My grief was full-time, but so was the business of death.

Once I returned to Nashville, that strange duality continued. Every day became a project. I carried folders, notepads, legal documents, and forms all tucked into Danny's favorite briefcase, the one I had recently gifted him. That briefcase, once carried with pride by my husband, became my daily companion. It was my new purse of choice, not for fashion, but for function. It held my whole life now.

In many ways, I believe the first year of widowhood passed in a haze, but it wasn't a useless haze. It was God-filled with paperwork. That paperwork, although frustrating, overwhelming, and often suffocating, gave me something to focus on. It gave my mind a mission, my days a reason to get dressed and get moving, and the need to keep going. I wanted everything, every single detail to be perfect for my Danny. Even in death . . . especially in death.

So, I functioned, heavily medicated by my doctor's orders. I was emotionally shattered and spiritually gasping, but I functioned. In that space, something else happened. I started to write what I couldn't speak. I didn't plan it; I didn't sit down with the intention of crafting a memoir. I simply began to journal. At first, it was just to keep track of what had to be done: "Call the life insurance company." "Request death certificates." "Send rent payment." Somewhere along the line, the entries became more emotional: "I miss his voice." "Why did this happen?" "God, are you still here?"

Over the next five years, I filled in more than 20 journals. Some entries made no sense, just scribbles of emotion, fragments of thought, and cries in ink. Others were clear, honest, and bold. Some days I wrote in the evenings to unload the weight of the day. Other times, I wrote first thing in the morning to prepare my soul for what the day might bring. I've looked back at those pages many times. They tell the story of a woman falling apart and finding her way again, one line at a time.

If you are grieving and walking through a storm of loss or pain, I urge you with my whole heart to start journaling. Don't worry about grammar. Don't worry about structure. Don't worry if it makes sense. Just write. Write what hurts. Write what heals. Write what confuses you. Write what you can't say out loud. Your soul still gets the message, and your heart still gets the relief. Some things can only be released through writing, and I'm still journaling my life's journey today.

JOURNAL ENTRY

"You're an inspiration,"
is what I've been told repeatedly.
Okay.
Thanks.
But I'm not trying
to be an inspiration.
I want to be
a wife
to Danny.

The Weight of Being "The Strong One"

There is a point where the silence grows thick, and the mask of composure starts to slip. There's a quiet kind of grief that doesn't wail or break things. It just sits in your chest like a large stone, while you go on folding laundry, answering emails, and making food you don't even want to eat. It's the kind that people don't see because you've learned to function too well. You've learned to smile in pictures and show up dressed, eyebrows done and voice steady, even when your heart is barely hanging on.

I've been the strong one for so long that it became my identity. Strength became my way of proving that I was okay, even when I wasn't, that I was "moving forward," even when I hadn't taken a real breath in days, and that I was "healing," even when I hadn't let myself be held. But here's the hard truth: Strength unchecked can become a cage. Behind my strength was a deep, unmet need to just be, not inspire, not overcome, not lead, just be messy, soft, angry, weeping, and human.

I thought falling apart would make me weak. If I collapsed, no one would be there to catch me, or worse, the world would keep spinning without me, and I would vanish in my own absence. I've learned that when you're always the strong one, no one offers to carry you. It's not because they don't love you; it's because they don't know you need it. You've trained them to think you're fine. That is a weight you were never meant to bear alone. Grief taught me this, not gently, but with fire. It stripped me of the illusion that my value is tied to my composure. It showed me that vulnerability is not a luxury; it's a necessity. A life without it isn't life. It's performance. It's pretending.

I gave myself permission to stop being the strong one, at least for a while. I laid it down, gently, but with finality. I let the silence swallow me. I let the sobs come when they came. I let people see me in the in-between, and slowly, I found that I was still whole, still worthy, still here, and maybe more alive than I'd ever been.

JOURNAL ENTRY

"Redefine what it means to be strong.
It takes strength to tell people you're
hurting.
It takes strength to say you need support.
It takes strength to ask someone
to prop you up for a while
because you're having a hard time
doing it on your own.
THAT'S STRENGTH."
— Pamela Booker

The Season of Being Unapologetically Selfish

But, I'm not a selfish person.

I'll never forget the words my spiritual mentor spoke to me the day we received the news that my husband had transitioned. Her voice, slow and sure in that southern drawl, wrapped itself around my name like a blanket. She said, *"Malika . . . this is bigger than you, and as you begin this journey, this is your time to be unapologetically selfish."*

At the time, that word hit me sideways, "Selfish?" I remember thinking, *But I'm not a selfish person.* It didn't make sense to me then, but oh, how my perspective has changed. Like many, I grew up believing that the word "selfish" meant lacking consideration for others, that it was self-centered, unkind, unbecoming, but grief flipped that understanding on its head. In my deepest valley, I realized that if I did not choose myself, I would not survive.

I came to see that being selfish in grief was not about ignoring others, but it was about honoring the very breath in my body. It was about giving myself permission to say "No" without an apology, to rest when my soul cried out for rest, and to protect my peace like my life depended on it, because it did. Now, I see intentional selfishness as a radical act of survival. I see it as normalizing the need to prioritize yourself in a world that constantly demands your emotional labor, even when you are broken.

Grief is intensely personal. It's selfish work. There's that "S" word again; I became selfish in the best way . . . I started honoring my emotions. I set boundaries without explaining myself. I allowed myself to rest when I was weary. I forgave my mistakes. I sought therapy. I joined support groups. I spoke kindly to myself. If that is what selfish looks like, then yes, I am selfish, Boldly, Unapologetically, and Gracefully.

Through those sacred, selfish choices, I honored God, the very one who created me. As I reflect now, I realize HE was with me the entire way, dropping what I like to call "God Nuggets" along the path, clues that reminded me I wasn't lost; I was simply shedding.

This is my redefined truth: Selfish is not neglect. Selfish is self-preservation. Selfishness is soul-care. Selfish is choosing to live when grief tries to bury you alive, and from that place of selfishness came healing. From that place came wholeness. From that place came compassion for others who are grieving. So, if you are grieving anything or anyone, allow me to say this gently, but boldly: **GO BE SELFISH!** Your healing depends on it.

JOURNAL ENTRY

Happiness is a choice,
but some consider it selfish.
Oh well.
I'll be selfish.

Midnight Wanderings

When I made the decision to be unapologetically selfish, it wasn't some bold declaration. It was a survival response. I was drowning in a grief I couldn't name and didn't have the language to describe. There were nights when my body grieved louder than my voice ever could. I would find myself standing in the middle of a room, startled awake, realizing I had been sleepwalking again. Other nights, as my mother later told me, I would moan deeply in my sleep, sounds that seemed to come from a place far beyond words, as if my soul itself was aching. Grief was working its way through me in ways I couldn't control.

Looking back, I believe those moments were my body's way of releasing what my heart couldn't yet speak. Healing doesn't just happen in the mind; it moves through the body . . . sometimes in tears, sometimes in stillness, and sometimes in the form of midnight wandering we can't explain. Whether it was sleepwalking, moaning, journaling until dawn, or simply sitting awake in the dark, my body was doing what it needed to do to survive the storm. I knew only one thing . . . if I didn't prioritize myself, I wouldn't make it.

That first two years after Danny transitioned were hollow, heavy, and utterly disorienting, but it became the groundwork for what I now call my "selfish healing," where I began to take the first small, intentional steps toward wholeness.

Counseling was the first lifeline. My mother suggested a 6-to-10-week grief recovery program her church offered, and I remember thinking, *why not?* I didn't have anything left to lose. My mother and my sister came with me to every single session, never once leaving my side. That kind of love holds you steady, even when you're too broken to speak. And I didn't speak, not at first. For the first three or four sessions, I said absolutely nothing. I was still in shock, still bleeding internally from the emotional wreckage. I had no words, just tears and silence. Slowly, something began to shift. By the eighth session, I found myself leaning into the conversation, offering fragments of my experience, and connecting with the stories around me.

That safe group setting became the first place where I didn't have to pretend. It was also where I met Dr. Christal Pennic, the best grief counselor on this side of Heaven, who is now a close friend. She was the first person to suggest I move my body; shake the grief loose through dance. I didn't know it then, but that invitation would become a lifeline.

She welcomed me to a dance fitness class at the local community center, Mondays, Wednesdays, and Fridays—and I showed up. Some days I drug my feet. Other days I almost forgot the weight I was carrying, but every time I finished a class, something inside me felt a little lighter. My body was still here. My heart was still beating, and somehow, that was enough.

This first year of selfishness was defined by a few core things: therapy, exercise, rest, EFT Tapping, and loud, unrelenting, private grief.

When I returned home to Nashville from Texas, I moved in with my mother. I was heavily medicated and still under doctor orders, just to help me function under the weight of my trauma. I slept a lot. I stayed inside most days. I wasn't "getting better." I was surviving. And that was enough.

Every night, for nearly a year or maybe even two, I cried myself to sleep. The tears came like clockwork. There was no escaping them. Just as there was no escaping the weight that sat on my chest every morning at 5:23 A.M., reflecting the exact numerical time listed on Danny's death certificate, although the actual time of his transition was 5:23 PM. Like some cruel internal alarm clock, my body remembered numbers 5:23.

In the silence of those mornings, I would remember his words: *"Promise me you'll always smile with your amazing smile."* Some days, all I could manage was a half-smile. Other days, not even that, but his voice and his love remained my fuel.

There's one more truth I must share here because it matters: During the first two, maybe even three years, I didn't PRAY. It was not because I didn't love God; I did. I always have and always will. I was raised in church, I knew how to pray, and I had a strong prayer life before the loss. But after Danny died, I didn't have the words. I didn't have the strength, and truthfully, I didn't have the will. I only wanted to know, how could an intentional God allow this kind of devastation? How could a loving God intentionally take my husband, the man HE knew I had waited for, the man He had given to me, only to rip him away?" I was too broken to speak to that God and too wounded to pretend I wasn't angry or confused. So, I stayed silent. If I prayed at all, it was only because someone asked me to pray for them, but I never went to God on my own behalf, not during that time. I just couldn't.

If that's where you are right now, feeling distant from God, angry with him, and numb toward him, I want you to know, it's okay. The God I know, the one who loved me through that silence, waited for me. He didn't leave me. He didn't scold me. He didn't shame me. He restored me. In time, as healing crept back in, so did my prayers, not perfect ones, not polished ones, but real, honest, and gritty, and God met me there, right in the middle of my brokenness.

The early years didn't include a lot of smiling. They were raw. They were dark, but intentional. Every choice I made . . . every nap, every tear, every boundary, every dance, and every word I couldn't pray was a step toward reclaiming my life. So yes, I was selfish.

Healing didn't begin with a miracle. It began with permission, permission to rest. Permission to cry. Permission to stop pretending. Permission to pray. Permission to grieve selfishly.

It wasn't about thriving. It was about surviving, and every time I chose myself, over the pressure to be okay and over the expectation to bounce back, I made a sacred decision to live, not just exist, but LIVE!

"Sometimes the bravest thing you can do is let the world keep spinning while you sit still and catch your breath." – Morgan Harper Nichols

JOURNAL ENTRY

God and Danny blessed me with a home.
Today, I signed the paperwork to begin
building.
I'm humbled...
excited...
sad...
missing DANNY...
NERVOUS...
and in awe of this blessing
that has overwhelmed my heart.

Before the
walls, was
the Word.

BUILT WITH LOVE,
BY DTW

Blueprints and Broken Pieces

I think I'm ready.

Years two and three didn't come with a bright sunrise or a turning point. It came with soft shifts, less sleepwalking, more clarity, and a touch more strength in the mornings. There were fewer tears, but still tears. I was still grieving and still healing. I was still selfish, but now, I was building. It started with a feeling, a quiet nudge in my spirit. I told my mom, "I think I'm ready. I am ready to step into a space of my own, ready to begin something new. I am ready to build.

What many didn't know is that Danny had always dreamed of building me a home. We used to sit on the couch flipping through home magazines, critiquing layouts and materials, like it was our job. We'd binge home renovation shows, pausing to imagine where the couch would go, what color we'd paint the cabinets, and what kind of lighting would hang above the island. We dreamed out loud. After he passed, those dreams became part of the ache, but they also became part of the why. To honor him and to honor myself, I chose to build the home he never got the chance to build for me.

When I told my mom about my decision, she paused. I saw her eyes well up with tears. I thought it was just the emotion of the moment, but then she shared something that I'll never forget. Danny had spoken to her, in detail, about wanting to build me a home, about what he hoped it would include, and about how much he wanted to give me a space filled with love, light and warmth.

She hadn't told me before. Maybe she was waiting for the right time, but that day, standing on a dusty lot with nothing but dirt beneath our feet, she said, "This is the kind of place he dreamed of for you." As she spoke, we both felt it, God's presence and Danny's presence. That empty lot checked every box of what my husband had imagined. And wouldn't you know . . . it was the one I chose.

While the house was being built, I found a new routine. I'd visit the lot daily, sometimes twice a day . . . just to watch, to sit, and to breathe. There was something holy about watching it rise, frame by frame and board by board. I often sat across the street and just stared, as if I was watching someone put my soul back together in wood and brick.

Around that time, I started to pray again! Remember those early years, I hadn't said a word to God. My prayers had been replaced by silence, deep, heavy silence, that only grief can birth. As the fog began to lift, something in me longed to talk to God again. I didn't start with eloquence or long petitions; I started with whispers. Some days it was just, "Lord, help me breathe." Other days . . . only tears spoke for me. Prayer became my quiet return to life. It didn't erase the pain, but it began to steady me. As I started to rebuild my physical home, laying the foundation brick by brick, I realized that prayer was doing the same for my soul. It was the groundwork for everything that would follow.

For those who may not share my faith, or those who have turned away from it because of loss, I understand. Grief can shake even the strongest belief. What I found is that prayer isn't always about having answers or perfect words; it's about permission, permission to feel, to question, to weep, and to still reach for something greater than your pain. That reaching is what begins to restore the cracks that loss leaves behind.

I remember one day I had written out eight Scriptures on small slips of paper . . . the number eight symbolizing new beginnings. That morning, I knew they were scheduled to pour the concrete slab, and I felt deep in my spirit that this was my moment to set the foundation of my home, not just in stone, but on the Word of God. So, when I wrote them, it wasn't just an act of faith; it was an act of rebuilding. Every verse was a brick in the foundation of a life I wasn't sure I could live again. And yet, prayer made it possible.

As I pulled up, the cement truck arrived at the very same time. The crew jumped out, and I nervously approached them to explain what I wanted to do. To my surprise, they didn't dismiss me or rush me away. Instead, they leaned in, listening with compassion, and one even said, "Of course, we'll make sure you can do that." The crew planned to start pouring cement from the back of the house, but when I asked if

I could place the Scriptures at the front entryway, so every step into my home would be covered, they shifted their plans and began there, just for me.

I gently tucked those Scriptures into the soil, right where the entryway would be, whispering prayers over each one. The men stood quietly, giving me space as if they knew this was holy ground. When I was finished, one contractor placed his hand on his chest and said, "I admire your strength. You will always be in my prayers."

To this day, every time I walk up my breezeway and open the front door, I'm reminded that my home, my healing, my faith, and my future are literally built on a solid foundation. It was healing to witness something so broken, just dirt at first, become something structured and whole. It mirrored exactly how I felt inside scattered, undone, but slowly being rebuilt by a bigger force than I.

Good morning, Gorgeous!

Prayer Room

Good morning, Gorgeous!

One day, about three and a half years after Danny transitioned, that sense of joy was harder to reach. It was a heavy-heart day, the kind where grief just walks in, uninvited, and sits on your chest. I had been thinking about Danny's voice and his laugh, the way he'd say things that only made sense between us, and the thought hit me like a wave I didn't see coming. I will never hear his voice again. The finality of that truth felt unbearable. I decided to take a quick drive to the store, I let out a painful sigh while driving, a moan from a place too deep for words. I was just going to pick out some decorative pillows. That was it, just a quick errand, nothing emotional. However, grief doesn't care about your plans.

I walked the aisles, trying to hold it together and blinking away tears as I scanned shelf after shelf, and then, tucked between other pillows, one caught my eye. It said: Good Morning, Gorgeous. I froze. Those were the exact words Danny said to me every single morning. Not, Hey, Baby. Not, You look nice. No, every morning it was, "Good morning, Gorgeous."

And there it was, stitched into a throw pillow, staring back at me like a message sent straight from Heaven. I lost it! Right there in the middle of the store, I slumped over the shopping cart and let it all pour out. The tears I'd been trying to hold back fell heavy and fast. I wept, not just for the man I missed, but for the beauty of that moment, the intimacy of that Divine wink, the gentleness of God, reminding me, I see you. I hear the ache. He's still with you. I'm still with you.

I clutched that pillow to my chest like it was made of gold. I searched desperately for more. I wanted ten, twenty, as many as I could carry, but there was only <u>one</u>. Yes . . . just one. It was enough because God, in His faithful and tender way, always knows how to speak directly to my heart, just like Danny did.

That pillow now lives in my prayer room. It sits quietly, but its presence is loud. It reminds me of a love that never dies, of a God who never left, and of a man who is somehow keeping his promise to make me smile. Please know that "our pillow" was more than décor. It was a love letter from Heaven, a God-nugget in cotton and thread, proof that Danny's love still reached me, and God's love never left me.

Grief breaks everything, but healing doesn't always begin with wholeness. Sometimes, it begins with bricks and pillows. Watching that house come together gave me more than a home; it gave me hope. It reminded me that even when everything feels like ruins, God is still building. Even in the silence, he's still speaking. Even in the sorrow, he's still sending signs. The foundation of my healing wasn't just laid in therapy, fitness, or rest; though, those things were holy. It was also laid in trust. That what was broken could be rebuilt. I was still worthy of a "Good morning," even on the hardest days.

As the house took shape, so did my desire to fill it with peace, with intention, and with things that made me feel loved, seen, and safe. Decorating became more than a task; it became therapy. Every picture I hung, every pillow I fluffed, and every detail I chose felt purposeful and even joyful, as though I was designing a space where my spirit could finally exhale. After weeks of carefully curating each corner, I had finally arranged the home in a way that brought me a sense of calm. I thought I had created the perfect balance between memory and newness, a place that felt like "us," while still giving room to heal.

I had intentionally set several pictures and special items exactly as they had been in our Texas apartment. It was my way of holding on to a piece of normalcy in a world that had been turned upside down. One day, I came home and immediately noticed that my housekeeper, with the best intentions, had moved everything. The moment I saw the changes; I had a complete meltdown. It felt like the fragile order I had created was undone, and in my grief and pain, I fired her on the spot.

Looking back, I realized this was grief speaking, not I. When you're walking through deep loss, it's so important not to let your emotions run you. That's an easy thing to say, but not easy to do when your heart feels broken in a thousand pieces. In time, with much healing, much counseling, and a huge apology, I rehired my housekeeper. Today, I'm grateful for her patience and grace, because that moment taught me that healing isn't about perfection; it's about progress. Grief can make the smallest disruptions feel like the biggest heartbreak, but each misstep, each stumble, is still part of the journey. Let's embrace the lesson here: Extend grace to yourself, and to others because healing isn't linear, but it is possible.

What I know for sure is this . . . You will have moments when your emotions get the best of you. You will say and do things you wish you could take back, and that's okay. Those moments weren't meant to define you; they were meant to refine you. Healing is not about holding everything together. It's about learning to breathe again, learning to forgive yourself, and finding the strength to keep moving forward. If I could extend grace to myself in that moment and circle back to make things right, then so can you. That's the beauty of this journey, we are stronger, wiser, and more resilient than grief ever wants us to believe.

When life shatters, rebuilding often begins beneath the surface, at the foundation. For me, it was eight Scriptures buried under concrete. For you, it may look completely different.

JOURNAL ENTRY

My mind still thinks of you.
My heart still holds a place for you.
My soul knows you're at peace.
I thank God for having had you.
You will always be remembered.
Rest well, Dannyboy.

When the Haze Lifts

This is your life now.

They never tell you about the haze. In the beginning, you move through death like a body without a soul, breathing, functioning, filling out forms, making calls, planning funerals, but not really feeling. The weight of it all is too much, so your spirit steps back while your body goes through the motions. Looking back . . . I believe that was God's Mercy. I believe God allows the haze intentionally, because facing the full weight of what happened too soon would have broken me mentally.

Year three, the haze began to lift, and with its lifting came the sharp sting of finality: Danny wasn't coming back, not in a dream, not in a phone call, and not in some miraculous twist. He was really gone, and that reality hit deeper than the initial shock ever could. There's a strange kind of pain that comes when reality fully arrives. It doesn't scream; it settles. It takes up residence in your chest. It whispers, "This is your life now." It dares you to keep breathing through it.

You might think a funeral would mark the end, but the heart doesn't understand ceremony; it understands absence, and in year three, that absence felt louder than ever. The grief became quieter, but it also became clearer. There was no more hiding in distractions. I was fully awake inside my pain.

I didn't stop counseling. In fact, I leaned in harder. I moved through multiple programs, one after another, not because the first wasn't enough, but because I knew this healing was going to take layers. I wasn't interested in just appearing okay. I wanted to be whole. I needed to be whole. And somewhere in this third year, I realized something important: Healing is a choice. Grief isn't, but healing is. Every day I showed up for myself in counseling, in journaling, and in moments of solitude, I was choosing to heal.

I began writing more, not just scribbles in notebooks, but honest, open letters to God, to Danny, and to myself. I poured out the things I couldn't say out loud, the fears, the memories, the anger, and the gratitude. There was something about seeing the words on the page that made them easier to carry. It was like I was giving weight to my pain, but I was also giving it somewhere to go.

It was selfish grief that led me here . . . the kind of sacred selfishness that allowed me to turn inward long enough to listen to my own soul. In that quiet, I found space to release. The same solitude that once felt heavy became the soil where healing began to take root. What I once thought was withdrawal was really preservation. What I once labeled as selfishness was survival.

Giving myself permission to grieve my way, to write, to weep, and to sit still was how I learned that healing isn't loud or pretty. It's honest, and it was in that honesty, through ink and tears, that I finally began to breathe again.

JOURNAL ENTRY

Valentine's Day is fast approaching.
I know I will be missing my love,
so God, please give me strength
just to get through it.
I finally ordered my memorabilia pillow
honoring Danny.
I can't wait to see it.
I'm going to go to sleep...
hopefully.
I don't sleep much nowadays.

A BIG AND QUIET GOD

A Big and Quiet God

He was sitting in it with me.

One night during this season of my grief journey, I found myself feeling extremely lonely and remembering a trip to Washington, D.C. as a child. I was maybe four or five years old, staring up at the enormous Lincoln Memorial. I remember being so small in its presence, marveling at the size, the posture, and the calm strength of it, really wishing I could climb into his lap.

In years three and four of my grief, I kept going back to that image. I'd close my eyes and imagine that statue was my God, my Lord and Savior, Still, Strong, Unshakeable. I, this broken, grieving woman, climbing up into His lap, like a child . . . not to pray, not to plead, but just to rest. That image held me in ways words could not, because when the haze lifted, I needed more than just therapy and journaling. I needed to be held.

I didn't need a sermon, I needed stillness. In those moments, I wasn't looking for answers. I wasn't even sure I could handle any. I just wanted to know that God was still there, that in my quiet unraveling, I hadn't been abandoned. Somehow, in that sacred silence, I began to feel Him, not in booming revelations, but in the breath between sobs, in the warm tears that softened the sharp edges of my sorrow. He wasn't solving my grief; He was sitting in it with me. And that was enough.

I learned that a big God doesn't always speak loudly. Sometimes He shows up in hushed mercies, a stranger's smile, a scripture whispered in memory, a morning where the ache is just a little less sharp. I started to believe again, not in the promise that pain would vanish, but in the truth that I didn't have to carry it alone. My God wasn't far away or offended by my doubts. He was expansive enough to absorb them and gentle enough to cradle me through them. And that image, the Almighty, holding space for my heartbreak, became my sanctuary.

Choosing Community Over Solitude

Even though I was coming alive again in some ways, there were still things I couldn't face. Silence was one of them. Solitude felt too loud, too sharp, and too empty. I followed my mother and sister around like a shadow. Wherever they were, I was close by, tagging along to functions, meetings, and errands. I didn't need to say much. I just needed to be near someone. There was safety in their presence. There was purpose in their movement.

In those moments of company, I was still protective of my space, selfish in a tender, necessary way. I learned that healing required discernment. My heart was still mending, and not every atmosphere could hold that kind of fragility. So, I moved gently with my "Yes's" and my "No's", careful about where I placed my energy, and with whom I shared my words. It wasn't distance; it was preservation. It was wisdom birthed from pain. Slowly being around people began to feel less like hiding and more like living.

Somewhere in the middle of all this healing, I met a few women who would change my life. Most of us were widows, brought together through therapy sessions and grief programs. We had different stories, but the same ache. There were different personalities with the same silence at night.

We bonded over tears at first, but what kept us connected was something deeper, our husbands' love for music and the arts. Every single one of our husbands, or significant others, adored music and the arts in some form, so we decided that we would honor them by continuing to live with music and art in our lives, concerts, plays, live jazz sets, and musicals. Whatever our schedules allowed, we went. We clapped. We cried. We laughed. We danced.

We call ourselves "The Winning Widows," not because we won at grief, but because we had chosen life. We chose friendship. We chose healing. We chose joy, even in its absence, and in choosing that, we began to rediscover our own rhythm. To this day, we still gather, still sing, and still share. We've learned to smile again, real smiles. And we carry our husbands and significant others with us, not as weight, but as witnesses.

As much as I loved the "Winning Widows" and the bond we shared, I knew deep down that I could not be the only widow still searching for healing and community. Something in me stirred to create a space not just for myself, but for others walking this same road. So, I decided to host a day party for widows. It was nothing like a funeral or a grief circle. No, this was going to be different. I wanted it to be a celebration of resilience and a safe space where women could cry, if they needed to, but they could also laugh, exhale, and feel whole for a day. I reserved a beautiful hotel space and had it catered. We had music, good food, and a welcoming atmosphere that felt more like a spa retreat than a grief gathering.

I brought in a masseuse because touch has a way of relaxing the soul. I invited someone to speak on financial stability because many widows find themselves suddenly navigating finances alone. I even brought in hairstylists, makeup artists, and boutique vendors, selling purses, jewelry, and all the pretty things that remind us that we are still women deserving of beauty and joy. We played games, shared stories, and, while tears were certainly shed, they were tears of release, of connection, and of finally feeling understood.

The day ended with something powerful, a balloon release. Each of us wrote our husbands' names or a personal message on a balloon. Together, we stepped outside, prayed, and let them rise into the sky. Watching those balloons drift upward felt like sending love notes to heaven, and in that moment, something lifted inside each of us. That day was unforgettable. It brought me to a new level of healing, simply by creating space for others to heal too.

That's the truth about grief and community, sometimes, if you can't find the community you need, you must create it. In doing so, you'll find your people, those who will walk the long road of healing with you. Some of the women who attended that day are still my healing circle today.

Then, something unexpected began to happen. Out of those circles, doors started to open for me to speak publicly about grief. Let me be clear. I have never loved public speaking. It wasn't something I ever pursued. Somehow, invitations kept coming, asking me to share my story, to speak to widows, to churches, to support groups, and to anyone navigating loss. At first, I was hesitant. I didn't think my journey was anything spectacular, except for the fact that Jesus carried me through it. However, each time I spoke, I could humbly feel God moving, not just in me, but in those listening.

My community expanded from intimate circles with widows to large gatherings where I was given the microphone. God continued to grow my reach and surround me with people who were also hungry for hope. It was never about me; it was about healing. Healing is possible, but it is also a choice. Each time I chose to step forward, whether to host, to speak, or simply to share, God met me there and multiplied it into something bigger than I ever imagined.

Grief can be one of the loneliest journeys you'll ever walk, but it doesn't have to be. Sometimes healing comes from being with others who truly understand, and sometimes it comes when you take the brave step of creating the very community you need. It doesn't have to be perfect. It doesn't have to be big. It could be a coffee with another widow, a support group at your church, or a circle of friends willing to simply sit in silence with you. Healing happens in safe spaces where we are seen and not judged. You don't have to grieve alone. Your people are out there. If you can't find them, don't be afraid to create them.

Finding community didn't mean that my season of selfishness had ended; it meant it had evolved. The same sacred selfishness that once caused me to withdraw was the very thing that positioned me to receive this circle of women. In choosing to protect my healing, I made space for God to bring the right people into it. Every boundary I set, every "No" I whispered, and every quiet night I spent tending to my heart were preparing me for this moment, to give from a place that wasn't empty.

Selfish grief has taught me how to pour into myself first so that when I found the "Winning Widows" and others, I could show up whole, not hollow. What began as a personal survival strategy became the foundation for shared strength. We weren't women broken beyond repair. We were women rebuilt through boundaries, prayer, and the courage to be unapologetically selfish long enough to heal.

Carrying Legacy

What gave me the push to move forward was the decision to create a legacy for my husband. Love doesn't end with loss; it transforms. And one of the most healing choices I made was to turn my grief into something that would outlive me. That's when I decided to establish an endowment at our beloved alma mater, Lane College in Jackson, Tennessee, where Danny and I both attended. Today, there is a scholarship in his honor: The Danny "Dannyboy" Terrell Williams Memorial Scholarship.

I remember sitting down to create the criteria for the students who would receive this scholarship. It wasn't just about financial support. It was about making sure Danny's spirit, values, and love for people lived on through each young person chosen. Even now, every time I meet or hear about a student who benefits from it, my heart swells with pride. To this day, people sow into Danny's endowment fund, some monthly, some weekly, and others spontaneously, when moved to give. Each donation reminds me that Danny's legacy continues to inspire, continues to serve, and continues to make room for the next generation of leaders. There is unspeakable joy in knowing that through this endowment, we are not only honoring his love for Lane College but also pouring into the lives of students the very thing Danny's heart always desired.

The endowment was only the beginning. I knew there were other ways I wanted to honor Danny to make sure his name wasn't just remembered but celebrated in the places he loved most. Basketball was one of Danny's greatest loves. He wasn't just good. He was one of the best players Lane College ever had . . . a fact proven not only by my bias as his wife, but by his induction into the Jackson County Hall of Fame/MVP, 1991. His love for the game was undeniable, and so was his impact on the court.

We used to joke about it often. I was a cheerleader during our college years, and he was, of course, the basketball star. He would always tease me, saying, "The cheerleaders got new uniforms every year, but the players had to keep wearing those same old musty jerseys year after year." I would laugh and tell him he was just complaining. We'd go back and forth, playfully debating who worked harder, the basketball players or the cheerleaders. And of course, I always told him we all knew the real answer to that. Lol!

In his honor, I met with the Lane College Athletic Department and basketball coaches to propose something close to my heart, purchasing brand new jerseys for the team, but I had one request. Each jersey had to bear the letters **"DW"** at the nape of the neck, a subtle, yet powerful reminder of Danny Williams. The coaches and staff were not only receptive, but they were also moved. They embraced the idea with gratitude and promised that his initials would live on with the team. The presentation took place during one of our fiercest rivalry games against LeMoyne-Owen College. At halftime, I had the honor of presenting the jerseys to the team in front of alumni, fans, family, and friends. That night, the Mighty Dragons took the court in those brand-new jerseys, with "DW" stitched proudly into each one of them, and in true Danny fashion, they didn't just wear them, they won the game. It was a close, hard-fought, thrilling rivalry game, and the Dragons came out victorious.

Each time the Mighty Dragons take the floor in those jerseys, Danny's name lives on, not just in the fabric of the game, but in the heartbeat of a college he adored. That night, as the crowd cheered and the team secured the victory, I knew it was bigger than just a win on the court. It was a win for Danny's legacy, stitched into every uniform, carried by every player, and celebrated by a community that loved him.

In many ways, it was my season of selfishness that became the soil for selflessness. The time I spent tending to my own brokenness, protecting my peace, guarding my space, and choosing what and who poured into me, wasn't about shutting the world out. It was God's way of restoring what was left of me so that I could give again, but this time, with purpose. Out of that sacred solitude came clarity, and out of that clarity came a calling . . . to carry Danny's name forward, not from a place of emptiness, but from overflow. What began as my simply trying to survive became my offering to the world, a selfless act born from a season of necessary selfishness.

What I've learned through this is that legacy can be built in many ways. For me, it looked like scholarships and jerseys. For you, it may look entirely different. Maybe it's creating a tradition, starting a fund, planting a garden, or simply living in a way that reflects their values. There is no one way to honor a loved one, **only your way**, and when you find it, you'll know. It will feel like love, continuing its journey through you.

JOURNAL ENTRY

I finally saw a red cardinal today.
They say when you see a cardinal,
the person you've lost
is thinking of you.
This blessed me
and made my shattered heart smile.
I miss DANNY every minute
of every day
and often wonder
if he's forgotten about me.

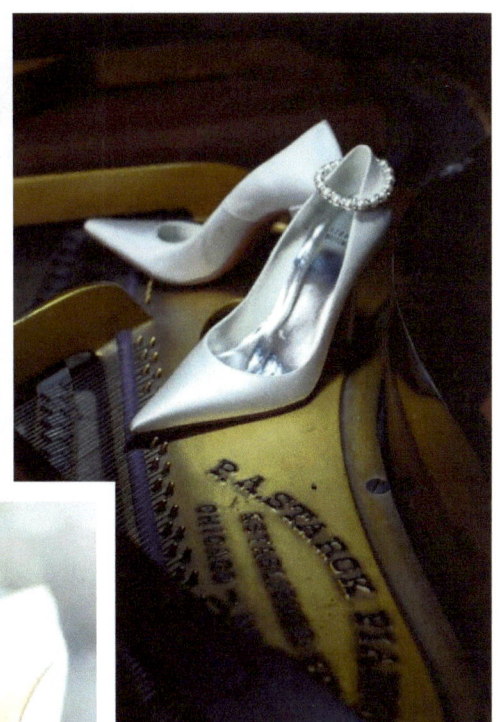

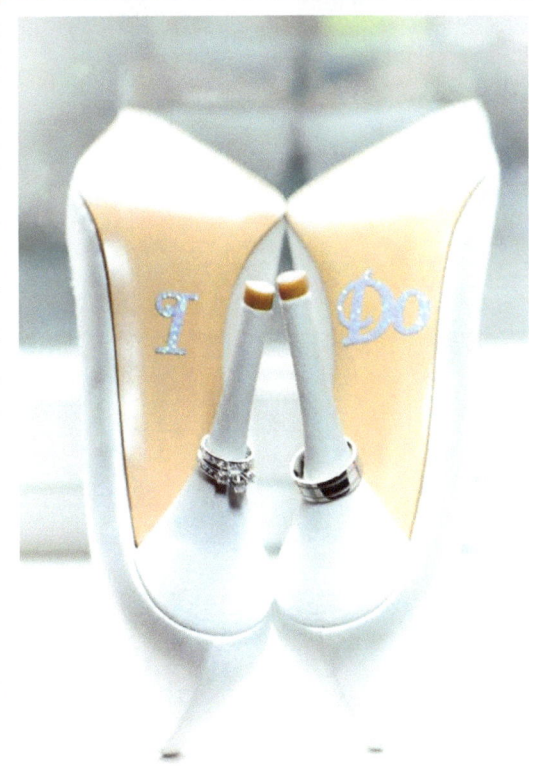

Symbols of Healing

Symbols of Healing

After Danny's endowment and jerseys were established, I found myself asking, *"What about me?" "What about my healing?"* I had given so much energy to keeping Danny's legacy alive, and I wanted to, but there came a point when I realized that part of honoring him meant also honoring myself. His love for me was never meant to leave me stuck in sorrow. His love wanted me to live.

I began to take small, but intentional steps, toward more healing. One of the first things I did was donate my wedding gown, veil, and other accessories to "Brides for a Cause," a nonprofit organization that collects and resells wedding dresses to raise funds for charity. Proceeds support various local and national women-focused charities. Letting go of that dress wasn't easy. It was the dress I wore when I said, "I do" to my forever love. Instead of sitting in my closet, collecting dust, I wanted it to breathe life into someone else's story. It was my way of giving another bride the chance to experience joy on her special day. In letting it go; I also let go of a little bit of pain and made room for a new layer of healing.

Years later, another symbol of my healing came through my wedding rings. For the longest time, well into year six or seven, I continued to wear them just as they had been given to me, the engagement ring and the wedding band. For a while, it was my comfort. I love jewelry, but this wasn't just jewelry. It was us. It was Danny's promise, his love, and his presence on my hand every single day. As time passed, what once brought me joy began to feel heavy. Every glance at my left hand reminded me not only of what I had, but also what I had lost. So, I made the difficult, but necessary decision, to redesign my wedding rings.

I took it to a trusted jeweler and explained my heart. I told him I wanted my ring to still capture the essence of the love Danny, and I shared, but I also wanted it to spark joy again. I wanted it to be a conversational piece, something that when people noticed, I could tell the story, not just of loss, but of love, of resilience, of still choosing to live. The jeweler listened carefully, and together we created something new. I moved the ring to my right hand, not as a symbol of the end of something, but as a new beginning. Every time I look at it now, it doesn't just remind me of Danny's proposal or our wedding day. It reminds me that love never dies, that healing is possible, and that even from something once broken, beauty can be made again.

Grief often leaves us clinging tightly to physical things, clothes, jewelry, photos, or even the smallest trinkets because they carry the weight of memory. That's okay. Those objects become anchors in the storm, but there may also come a time when you feel called to reimagine what those symbols mean for you, maybe it's donating something, so it can bring joy to someone else; maybe it's redesigning a piece of jewelry so that it brings light instead of heaviness, or maybe it's simply moving an item from one place to another, giving it a new purpose in your life. There is no right or wrong way, **only your way.**

I encourage you to take a moment and look around at the tangible pieces of your loved one's story that are still with you. Ask yourself, do they still bring me comfort, or do they bring me sorrow? And if it's sorrow, ask yourself, could I reshape them into something that helps me heal?

Remember, healing doesn't erase love. Healing redesigns it, so you can carry it forward in a way that brings life, not just loss.

JOURNAL ENTRY

Today felt like closure
and Rebirth
all at once.
I left with some tears...
yes...
but also with a sense of freedom
I hadn't thought possible.

There is no wrong way. There is **only your way.**

ΚΑΨ

"DANNYBOY"

JOHN 3:15

DANNY TERRELL WILLIAMS

NOV. 5. 1967 – DEC. 12. 2014

BELOVED HUSBAND FATHER SON BROTHER

Your Way

I have never considered myself a "gravesite girl." Even growing up, cemeteries never brought me comfort, and when it came to my husband's passing, that truth remained. Over the past ten years, I can honestly say that I've only visited Danny's gravesite maybe five times.

The final time was on December 12, 2024. If you pay attention to that date, you'll notice it's the very day Danny transitioned. Ten years later, I felt something stirring in me. I had reached a level of healing that made me feel I needed to go, just once more. It was not to dwell there and not to carry guilt for not going before, but simply to release, to close a chapter.

I never felt the need to go often, because deep down I always knew Danny wasn't there. His body was, but he wasn't. Still, on this day, I knew I had to go, and I wasn't alone. My dear college best sister-friend, Angela Mathis, flew in from California just to be with me for this visit. Her presence was such a gift. Unbeknownst to me, she quietly captured a few tender photos of that sacred moment. Looking back now, I see how her thoughtfulness created a memory I'll carry forever.

That visit brought me closure, a release. It reminded me that healing does not look like one thing, one place, or one action. For me, going to the gravesite that day was necessary, but so was letting it be my last. Even in the stillness of that final visit, God's presence carried me forward, and healing belongs to Him as much as it belongs to me. I left the gravesite that day with tears in my eyes, but freedom in my soul.

I am often asked by others navigating grief if they should visit the gravesite. My answer is always the same: "There is no "should." If going brings you peace, then go. If it brings heaviness, then don't. Do not let anyone make you feel guilty or question your love, if visiting the gravesite is not your way. Here's the truth: The person you love is not there. You do not earn an award for grieving the way society expects you to grieve. There is no right way. There is no wrong way. There is **only your way**.

Light Finds You in the Dark

Grief is heavy, but I would be remiss if I didn't pause to acknowledge the overwhelming kindness that covered me in my darkest season. Whether I was in Texas or Tennessee, I was met time and time again with gestures of compassion from people who knew me well, and others who barely knew me at all. There were flowers that brightened rooms I no longer wanted to enter, and I received teddy bears that were sent with love . . . one, tenderly named Manny, which is a blend of Malika and Danny, still rests with me today. Friends sent journals for me to spill my heart into, letters filled with words I didn't have the strength to write myself, edible arrangements when food was the last thing on my mind, and generous donations to Danny's endowment fund, so his legacy would live on.

The greatest gift came not in things, but in presence. I had friends who would literally just come and sit with me. They didn't need to fill the silence or fix what couldn't be fixed. They just showed up. In grief, I learned it isn't perfection that matters; it's presence.

I write this as a wholehearted "Thank you" to those I can recall in vivid detail and to those whose kindness I may have overlooked in the dense haze of grief. Your love was light. Your gestures, your words, your silence, and your time were reminders that I was not alone, even when my world felt like all the lights had gone out.

Danny would tell me repeatedly, all he ever wanted was to see me happy, and though he had to leave, I've finally reached a place where I can embrace that. I know he would want me to enjoy every moment of life. So, I've decided to live out the legacy of that love and be over the moon happy every day.

If you are grieving anything or anyone, allow me to encourage you to, GO BE SELFISH!!!

Messages from Danny's coworkers

Thank you for including us. I had only worked with Danny since August of last year, but we (me, him and Ronnie) formed our own little bond, looking out for one another. We enjoyed his spirit here and he will... is still missed. Because life, and as we know it, death, can sometimes be sudden, we have to "cherish life" as you say. His story caused me to make some adjustments in my life. Since that day, I have texted my two sons daily with a good morning and before my head hits the pillow, a message of love to them. Again, thank you for allowing us to reflect alongside you at the balloon release memorial. — Daniel

I've never seen Danny so happy and in-love the way he was with you! I think of him often an miss him very much! Each time I se you, I see him smiling with so much love he has for you!!! I know that I only met you once before you married but I knew Danny and the way he lit up when he spoke of you! He's always watching over you and wants only the best for you and for you to find and be as happy as ever possible...whatever that is for you!!! Proud of how strong you've been these past 11 years! Wishing you all the best!!!!! — Stormy Price

Malika...every time we show one of Danny's training videos at work, it is like he's there with us! Not a single day goes by in the studio where someone doesn't talk about Danny. He was at the heart of so many of our skits...and was so important to us! - Denise

Malika, I pray that God will continue to comfort you, your heart, and strengthen you as the days come and go.

Messages of Encouragement for Malika

I share the same sentiments echoed in this response thread. I was there as you know. While difficult, you took on the pain and walked us through it as a source of encouragement.

Please take a bow... Rev. Dr. Cathy Wilikins Moffitt

Thank you for living it out in "full living color". Your tenacity, strength, perseverance and love is both admirable and courageous. I love you and I am incredibly proud of you.

Good morning, Malika! I hope all is well with you. I'm in Nashville for work and you were on my mind. Just wanted to say that you helped me so much on my grief journey and poured into me with your love, support and prayers. It has helped me to heal throughout my journey. Thank you gorgeous - Reiko Reliford

So beautiful! I am so proud and happy for the love that you and Danny shared.
Thank you for doing the work to heal, live and for being transparent on this journey.
Candace Williamson

Danny, I'll miss your sweet spirit! When I found out you were marrying Malika I was soooooo happy for you two. Malika is carrying your legacy gracefully, like no other. Continue to rest in God's love. - Debbie Long

*Memories are God's
way of saying,
"Nothing beautiful is
ever lost."*

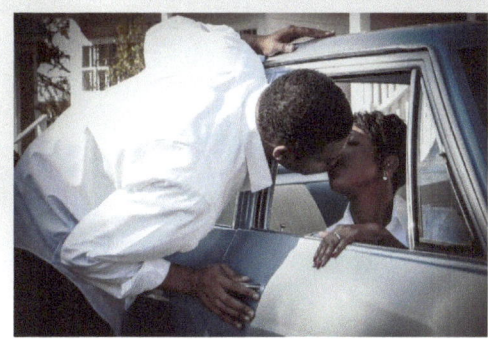

Back Row, left to right: Coach Ozell Williams, Damon Choice, John Davis, Mechalie Jamison, Charles Bell, Allen Bond, Kevin Wynn, Gerard Williams, Michael Farmer. First Row: Danny Williams, Wendell Quarles, Rodney Moody, Lamar Chapman, Andre Jordan, John Granberry, Roderick Hall.

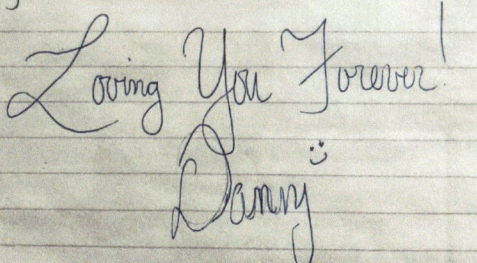

Baby, I simply wanted to write you to give you a small inkling of how much you have changed, enhanced and brightened my life. I will always LOVE YOU more than the mere words I've written on this paper or any token I've given to you. I LOVE YOU til God takes the last breath from my body.

Loving You Forever!

Danny

ACKNOWLEDGMENTS

To my mother, Ruth Wharton:
Your strength is my blueprint. Thank you for modeling grace,
resilience, and unshakable faith. Every page of this book carries your
support, your wisdom, your warmth, and your prayers.

To my sister, Sherrie Cooper:
Your unwavering support in the early days, when I was too fragile to
stand, too broken to speak, was my lifeline. Your protection, your
presence, and your covering were sacred gifts that helped hold me
together. I am forever grateful.

To my immediate and extended family and friends:
Whether it was a grief session, a phone call, a card, or a quiet text, your
love and encouragement became divine nudges. Thank you for
standing by me, believing in me, and reminding me to finish what God
had placed in my heart. This book is a testament to your faith in my
healing and your patience with my process.

To Lisa and Anthony Stevenson of LWI - Living with Intention
Publishing, and your amazing team:
Thank you for patiently and calmly walking me through the journey of
writing my memoir. You have no idea how many times I was ready to
give up, and yet each time, your encouragement whispered, "Push." I
did and I'm still pushing.

To my sensi editor, Valerie Payton:
Thank you for your keen eye and gentle precision. You didn't just edit
my words, you honored my voice, polished my pain, and brought
clarity to places where grief had once blurred the page.

hey there!

"What grief tried to silence, God resurrected into purpose and that purpose is to remind the world that life after loss is not only possible but also PROMISED!" Jeremiah 30:17

Malika Sabän Williams is a Master Certified Etiquette Consultant, public speaker, and the visionary founder of Excuse Me, Please Etiquette Company. Beyond her work in refinement and civility, Malika is a resilient woman who has walked through the depths of grief and emerged with strength, faith, and renewed purpose.

Her husband, Danny Williams, was the love of her life, and his passing just 14 months into their marriage reshaped her journey. Through pain, healing, and rebuilding, Malika has dedicated her life to encouraging others that life after loss is possible and joy after loss is real.

Malika's story is one of God's faithfulness. She credits HIM as the steady hand that carried her through her darkest nights and the source of the peace, courage, and healing she now walks in. She writes and speaks with the conviction that the same God who lifted her will lift others too, and she encourages every reader to trust that He can and will bring them through their own valley seasons.

Whether through her writing, her public speaking, or the communities she helps build, Malika's mission is clear: to remind others that they are not alone, that healing is a choice, and that legacy and love never die. She continues to honor Danny's memory through scholarships, community initiatives, and everyday acts of grace, while inspiring others to rise, rebuild, and redefine what it means to live fully after loss, anchored always by God's unfailing love.